Brass Performance and Pedagogy

Brass Performance and Pedagogy

Keith Johnson
University of North Texas

Upper Saddle River, New Jersey 07458

Library of Congress Cataloging-in-Publication Data

Johnson, Keith
 Brass performance and pedagogy / by Keith Johnson.
 p.cm.
 Includes index.
 ISBN 0-13-091483-5
 1. Brass instruments—Instruction and study. 2. Brass
   instruments—Performance. I. Title.

 MT418 .J64 2001
 788.9'193'071 —dc21   2001021981

Acquisitions editor: Christopher T. Johnson
Production editor: Laura A. Lawrie
Manufacturing and prepresss buyer: Benjamin D. Smith
Copy editor: Laura A. Lawrie
Editorial assistant: Evette Dickerson
Cover design: Bruce Kenselaar

This book was set in 12/14 Bembo by Laura A. Lawrie
and was printed and bound by Courier Companies, Inc.
The cover was printed by Phoenix Color Corp.

 © 2002, Pearson Education, Inc.
Upper Saddle River, New Jersey 07458

Printed in the United States of America
10 9 8 7 6 5 4 3 2 1

ISBN 0-13-091483-5

Prentice-Hall International (UK) Limited, London
Prentice-Hall of Australia Pty. Limited, Sydney
Prentice-Hall of Canada, Inc., Toronto
Prentice-Hall Hispanoamericana, S.A., Mexico
Prentice-Hall of India Private Limited, New Delhi
Prentice-Hall of Japan, Inc., Tokyo
Pearson Education Asia Pte. Ltd., Singapore
Editora Prentice-Hall do Brasil, Ltda., Rio de Janeiro

For Cecile, Andrea, and Stephen

Talent perceives differences, genius unity.
W. B. Yeats

Contents

X: Mouthpiece Playing   41

XI: The Warm-Up   45
         1. Breathing   47
         2. Mouthpiece Playing   48
         3. Lyrical Studies   48

XII: Slurring   51

XIII: Intonation   53

XIV: The Upper Register   57

XV: Endurance   61

XVI: Vibrato   65

XVII: Braces   67

XVIII: Teaching the Young Orchestral Player   71

XIX: Preparation   75
         Solo Playing   75
         Chamber Music Playing   77
         Large Ensemble Playing   78

XX: Taking Auditions   79

XXI: Playing High Pitched Instruments   83

XXII: Performance Anxiety   87

XXIII: Professional Ethics   91

         Index   93

Acknowledgments

I would like to thank the following for reviewing the manuscript:

Edmund Cord, Indiana University
Sande MacMorran, University of Tennessee
Dr. William Stowman, Messiah College
Dr. Thomas Tritle, University of Northern Iowa

I am grateful to my wife, Cecile, and my children, Andrea and Stephen, for their love and support, to Fr. Emmett Waits for his wisdom and friendship, and to David Monette, Jon Hansen, and Don Little, three of the finest colleagues one could hope to have. All these people have contributed more than I could ever adequately acknowledge.

Keith Johnson
Denton, Texas
August 15, 2000

Preface

Teaching is an art. It defies reduction to a set of rules or formulae. It is above all a supreme kind of communication between two people, the teacher and the student. Much time is wasted in debate over just what form this communication should take. Some advocate this method or that, one philosophy or another. Such arguments miss the point. Good teaching is art, not science, and any attempt to reduce it to pseudoscientific methodology is not only doomed to failure but speaks clearly as to the constricted thinking that even attempts such codification.

I have had the good fortune to know many excellent teachers during my career. As a student, I had several fine trumpet teachers, and as a college professor I have had the privilege of working with a number of outstanding colleagues, first at the University of Northern Iowa and later at the University of North Texas.

The teaching styles of these people have covered such a broad range as to lead me to the conclusion that good teaching defies analysis and narrow prescription. Fine teaching is easy to recognize, impossible to categorize. I have known fine teachers who behaved sternly with their students, and others who were permissive. I have known brilliant pedagogues who were models of organization, and others who practically had to be led to their studios.

There are qualities, however, that have been present in the work of all the really gifted teachers I have known. First, all have cared passionately about their subject. They have loved it, been possessed and at times consumed by it, and have manifested this passion throughout their careers. Second, they have been devoted to their students. This devotion may have been expressed as concern, irritation, sympathy, even anger. But it is real concern, the kind that says to the student that he or she is capable of meeting high standards and of learning and producing at a level that rejects academic or artistic compromise.

One of the most challenging aspects of teaching musical performance is that the subject demands immediate, clear, and public demonstration. There is no hiding place for the performer on the stage, and, likewise, none for the teacher. Our efforts are there for the world to hear. Such discipline is harsh but honest. It allows little room for charlatans, and it precludes resting on yesterday's accomplishments.

My interest in performance and teaching are as vigorous today as they were in my student days. Music itself and the students who pursue it are the inspiration for my enthusiasm. Music and its practitioners need no apologists; music needs only to be heard in order to inspire, console, or disturb.

One who teaches musical performance must never forget that the reason we do what we do and the very inspiration that will sustain a long career is the music itself. As a teacher, one must remember to return to music daily, to listen as well as to teach and play in order to keep purpose, quality, and meaningful direction in one's work.

Only the music, which drew us in at the beginning, provides the inspiration needed to continue to produce as players and teachers.

Introduction

This book is intended for persons who teach brass players. It is hoped that it will be of use not only to brass specialists but also to people whose own performance area is in another medium.

Many of the ideas expressed in this book are widely held by fine brass teachers, and no claim is made that the ideas are new or unique. Much of what is written is similar to what I have expressed in an earlier work, *The Art of Trumpet Playing*, as well as in numerous articles in various publications. The principal difference with this work is that whereas most earlier writings have been directed toward individual players concerned about their own performance, the present work is written for the teacher who deals with all the brass instruments. It is by intention of a more general pedagogical nature. This should not be construed to mean that the information is diluted, but rather that the topics are those common to brass instruments (and, I suspect, to many other areas of musical performance).

One of the serious weaknesses I observe in much brass instruction is what I call "over teaching"; that is, the seductive inclination to give the student as much particularized information as possible, often resulting in mental overload. Musical performance is not about the acquisition of extensive, highly specialized pieces of information but rather is about the acquisition of musical concepts (ideas) and the development of the corresponding skills necessary to give expression to those ideas. We are not scientists, and we are not teaching aspiring scientists (at least not in the specific context of musical performance). Rather, we are (we hope) creative artists helping others to learn how to participate in the creative process. Creative or conceptual thinking is fundamentally different from analytical thinking, and failure to understand the differences between the two modes of thought can have disastrous consequences for performers. More will be said in the early chapters of this book about developing creative thinking, how it can be taught, and how it differs from analytical thought.

The ideas expressed here are intended to serve teachers who deal with brass students at all stages of development. These ideas are those that I have used in more than three decades of teaching brass students. I have no pedagogical secrets to reveal, and I know of no shortcuts to success. I believe that good playing is the result of the successful acquisition of the fundamentals of playing and the continuous development of those fundamentals to the highest possible levels through years of conscientious practice. Anyone looking here for gimmicks or quick fixes will be disappointed. I do not believe in such approaches, and the finest teachers and players I know exemplify the view that basic skills and diligent work are the keys to success.

As brass players, we practice an art form that has not changed fundamentally for many centuries. We still need fine listening skills, good use of the breath and a singing, musical approach to our craft just as our professional ancestors did. These things take time and effort to acquire. We practice a noble and beautiful craft that demands our best efforts, and when properly developed, provides immense personal rewards that make the difficult challenges worthwhile for us and for our listeners.

I

The Art of Teaching

Teaching is an art, not a science. There are no exact rules, no foolproof formulae for successful teaching. There are as many good ways to teach as there are good teachers. After many years of working in universities and observing hundreds of teachers and students, I am convinced that no course of study can ensure success as a teacher if an innate talent is not present. Certainly good training can guide and develop those who have the gift and desire to teach, but no curriculum is so successful as to assure that its completion will automatically produce a fine teacher.

There are, however, qualities that seem present in most fine teachers. These qualities need not be manifest in similar proportions in every good teacher, but most people will remember their most influential teachers as having had these traits, often expressed in various forms.

The most important qualities any good teacher should possess are a thorough knowledge of the subject matter and a concern for the student's progress. I have seen many music teachers who were never very good musicians or who somewhere along their careers lost their love for music. Such people do serious damage not only because they fail to teach their subject well but also because by their very presence they teach that incompetence and/or indifference are acceptable.

To teach music successfully one must first be a good musician. Such musicianship can take many forms. The most obvious are as a performer, conductor, or composer, but teaching itself can take on a form of musical expression. Being a good musician (at least for the purpose of teaching) requires not only success in making music, but also a solid knowledge of musical styles, theory, and history. It also requires being a sophisticated listener. One should be deeply suspicious of so-called musicians who rarely attend concerts, listen to recordings, or fail to find other ways to stay active in music.

The acquisition of musical ideas should be a lifelong process. The finest musicians continue to grow, study, and learn throughout the longest of careers. Any teacher who ceases to study has forfeited the moral right to be a teacher.

An unfortunate occurrence in the music profession is the development of a cynical attitude on the part of some teachers. Most teachers, music and otherwise, are overworked, underpaid, and underrecognized. Frustration and bitterness sometimes result. The damage done by such attitudes is not limited just to the particular teacher. Students learn from what the teacher *is* as much as from what the teacher may say. In short, the fine teacher must be a thoughtful, devoted musician for whom the joys of music are obviously important.

The most successful teachers are those dedicated to the highest musical and academic standards in their own professional lives as well as in their expectations for their students. They settle for nothing less than the students' best efforts. They are uncompromising in what they expect from their students, and they are willing to do battle with inferior teachers, parents, and administrators rather than lower standards for the purpose of ease, personal advancement, or the convenience of serving a mindless bureaucratic system. A well-known newspaper columnist once remarked that he was deeply suspicious of any teacher who had not been fired at least once. In an age of indifference, physical comfort, and instant gratification, a demanding teacher is virtually a subversive. So be it. Teaching is about change, and the dedicated teacher's values are predicated on the importance of the subject matter and its value to the life of the student and society. It seems as good a place as any to take a stand.

II

Music as Metaphor

When I was a beginning teacher I considered it my goal and my responsibility to attempt to train each of my students to be a fine professional player. I soon learned from my students that this was a foolish, misplaced objective in many instances. While I have been fortunate enough to have many wonderful, sometimes outstanding students who have pursued successful performing careers, many of my students have taken careers that have led them in other directions. Many have become fine public school teachers (a rarer and much more needed breed than professional trumpet players), and many have chosen professions outside of music altogether. For a time I was troubled when students chose other fields because I believed the time we had spent working on their trumpet playing was wasted. I no longer hold that view. Rather, I have come to see the trumpet as a metaphor for other aspects of life. Whether that life is spent as a performer, a music teacher, or in a seemingly unrelated field, I firmly believe the lessons learned from performance and the intrinsic value of music are so great as to inform and shape any life in a genuinely enlightening way regardless of the specific career path.

Years ago I had a friend who was an exceptionally able businessperson. He started a company and built it into a moderate-sized corporation employing many people in offices throughout the country. During the course of a conversation he remarked to me that he really liked to hire employees who were former music students. At first I found this strange since his business in no way was connected to anything musical. He explained that he found music students to have much better self-discipline and a greater willingness to work hard than persons from most other backgrounds. He went on to say that he found former music students have the ability to take on individual responsibility as well as the ability to work well in group endeavors.

When I asked him about the music students' lack of specific training in business skills, he replied that it was of no concern. Any business will train its employees in the specific skills needed by that business. It seems that what most professions require are individuals who can think and act independently as well as function well with colleagues and who respond well to changing situations. People who are narrowly trained frequently lack the ability to adapt.

Good musical education should serve at least three laudable purposes. First and most obvious is that the student should become a more accomplished performer in accordance with his or her ambitions and talent. Second, the student should acquire a heightened awareness of the importance of aesthetic values and creativity far beyond the specific level at which he or she may actually play. The world has a great need for civilized, enlightened audiences who understand the importance of the enriching and humanizing effects of art. Third, student performers should learn that music is a metaphor for learning all the productive skills so essential to a meaningful life.

None of us teaches or plays in isolation. If what we do is to have genuine value we must understand that our art is both *timeless* and *relevant*, and we must convey to our students how our efforts as musicians relate to and impact upon all aspects of a worthwhile, civilized life.

III

Teaching the Young Brass Player

Playing a brass instrument can be both enormously rewarding and terribly frustrating. Certain amounts of both experiences are almost inevitable, but the approach employed by the teacher can have a decided influence on which experience is more prominent. To play a brass (or any other) instrument well involves long hours of dedicated practice supported by competent teaching. The best teaching is that which challenges and encourages the student by setting high (but not unrealistic) goals and that builds confidence, dependability, and the desire to continue to advance.

Such objectives, rather than being abstract, are very real and probably have more to do with the student's ultimate success than such physical properties as vital capacity, embouchure formation, or innate coordination. All students are inherently musical, at least to some degree, and the role of the teacher is to create a situation in which the student's talents are most completely developed.

One of the most persistent and difficult problems facing any teacher is that of establishing and maintaining high standards in the face of student apathy, parental pressure or neglect, and administrative red tape. Yet, the fastest way to lose a student's interest is to allow the goals set for him or her to sink to a mediocre level. Even the least talented student has some ability to distinguish among various levels of musical quality (in both performance and literature), and adhering to high musical standards will attract and retain more good students in the long run than will compromising musical integrity.

Even the youngest beginner can (and should be encouraged to) make judgments regarding musical values. In many situations it is assumed that musicality and creativity come about only after a certain level of technical competence has been acquired. While it is true that greater technical skills give one the freedom to be more expressive, it is also true that the beginning student's first lesson should be as much an attempt at playing expressively as it is an attempt to start the long road to technical mastery.

For brass students, two of the most important areas of their efforts, both initially and throughout their careers, are those of singing and listening. The greatest weakness in most young (and old) players is that they do not hear really well. No one is ever likely to become a successful musician without first developing the skill of listening, and one of the best ways to begin to develop listening skills is by singing. Perhaps a good suggestion for brass players is to join the choir as well as the band and orchestra and learn that the primary function of every musician is to "sing," either vocally or instrumentally. In order to sing well one must hear pitch, timbre, volume, diction (articulation), balance, and rhythm. These skills transfer quickly to instrumental performance.

A great problem for many brass students is that so much emphasis is placed on the mechanical aspects of performance (respiratory function, embouchure, etc.) that the student fails to grasp the larger musical goal to which these physical efforts are directed. In other words, the student needs to know how he wishes to sound before he tries to play. Singing and listening (to records, concerts, radio broadcasts) are as essential to musical development as listening to a spoken language is to learning to speak that language.

All this teaching, practicing, listening, and learning must be done in an atmosphere that stresses quality, musical values, and the satisfaction that comes from good music making. More emphasis needs to be placed on playing musical lines than on merely hitting correct notes. More compliments should be given for producing a beautiful, resonant tone than for squeaking out a high note of no musical quality, and at least as much effort should be directed to complimenting the areas in which the student has progressed as is given to pointing out errors or inadequacies.

Perhaps the most crucial physical area of concern for brass players is respiratory function. Good breathing is as necessary to the life of the sound as it is to the life of the player. Extensive theories pertaining to the teaching of breathing have been put forward over the years, some with more validity than others. Perhaps the most effective way to help students improve their breathing for purposes of brass playing is to simply tell the student to relax, breathe fully (I like to have students produce the sound "OH" when they breathe), and blow the air out in a full, free-flowing column, thinking airflow rather than force. Such words and phrases as "support" and "blow harder" are oftentimes misinterpreted so as to cause unwanted tension and restriction of the air.

Most aspects of good brass playing are so integral to a full, rich sound that developing a resonant, singing tone quality is of paramount importance. Such a sound inevitably and absolutely depends on a full, free approach to breathing guided by good listening skills. Once such a breath and sound have been acquired many features of the student's playing will show dramatic and continuous improvement. Range, endurance, intonation, even articulation, and embouchure function depend heavily on good airflow, and the best indication of efficient use of the air is the basic tone quality being produced.

Finally, let me urge all of those who teach brass instruments not to be overly concerned with the specific intricacies and technical nuances of the individual instruments. Many of the finest brass students come from teachers who are not themselves brass players. In fact, some of the most severe problems I have observed have been in students whose teachers were performers on the same instrument. There is always a danger of over teaching; that is, filling the student's mind with a cluttering array of technical information, often more fascinating than beneficial. A young student (or a performer of any age and experience) is much better served by thinking of a beautiful sound and a flowing musical line than by consciously attempting to manipulate the intricate workings of the embouchure or respiratory system.

It is far better in most instances to teach in accurate musical generalities than to burden players with unnecessary mechanical details. Performing musicians at every level of development should be engaged in the artistic rather than the scientific aspects of music, and the teacher's challenge is to help the student focus on the creative and expressive aspects of playing. Such a musical approach will ultimately achieve artistic success and technical accomplishments more quickly than an overly analytical approach.

More will be said later about many of these specific skills, but the teacher should always keep in mind that the goal is to teach *musical* performance. All other pedagogical decisions should be predicated on this overriding caveat.

IV

Listening

The most important skill any musician must develop is the skill of listening. Listening provides the means by which we acquire musical ideas and the means by which we evaluate our product. Any success we enjoy will be absolutely connected to the level of our listening skills.

We must learn to listen with accuracy, objectivity, and imagination. Unfortunately, much in contemporary culture works against acquiring perceptive listening. Banal music—on radio and television, in offices and elevators—actually teaches us not to listen. The purpose of such music in these examples is to mask other sounds (noise) or to subliminally influence our mood or behavior. Real music, by contrast, influences us, but its purpose is directly engaging and honest. We must strive not only to be aware of its presence but also to participate in it, to take it into our sensory memory and to call upon it when we are exercising our own capacity for creating music.

Many years ago, while presenting a clinic, I was asked by an instrumental music teacher whether there was one single piece of advice I could give that he could use to improve the trumpet players in his band. My response was quick, direct, and honest: "Have all your trumpet players join a choir." The voice is certainly the original (and perhaps the most sublime) musical instrument, and through it we can quickly ascertain if a player's mind really contains musical ideas. No musical sounds that are not first produced in the mind can be accurately and consistently reproduced. Having a student sing a passage is the quickest, most accurate way to ascertain if the student is actually able to hear the music.

The skill of listening should be introduced to brass players during the first lesson and improved upon every lesson thereafter. Every phrase should be sung by the student before being attempted on the instrument. Unless the player can accurately sing what is to be played, any correct results on the instrument are more accidental than intentional and are likely to be short-lived. By learning to hear (sing), the young student becomes product oriented (sound) rather than means oriented (mechanics).

If we wish to dramatically improve music teaching we need only require the daily practice of *solfège* at every level of musical study. Music must be heard, and the more accurately and imaginatively we hear it, the better we can reproduce it.

The vast majority of students have as their most serious and restricting problem the inability to conceive in their mind's ear how they wish to sound, and subsequently they are unable to assess accurately the sounds actually produced. A glaring example of this problem is demonstrated when a young player hears himself on a recording for the very first time. There is a vast discrepancy between how the student sounds and how he thinks he sounds. Creating a realistic awareness (objectivity) is one of the significant benefits of teaching listening. The ensuing result (after the shock wears off) is always one of improved performance. The most intransigent problem is the one the player cannot hear.

Much emphasis (usually too much) is placed on mechanical aspects of brass playing, often overloading the player's mind with information that precludes better listening and ultimately better production. Most mechanical responses occur naturally, efficiently, and dependably if the student simply focuses on the desired musical result rather than on trying to consciously control the complex motor skills that function below the level of conscious thought.

Mechanical problems often result from too much specific physical instruction and too little effort devoted to creating awareness of the desired musical product through creative musical listening. Physical skills are best learned when one attempts to imitate clearly understood goals. Such learning takes place through imitation; speech, walking, riding a bike, writing, and so on. All of these accomplishments are learned with some degree of success by all healthy individuals, and they are virtually always acquired with an absolute minimum of specific physical instruction.

Example and encouragement are two of the best methods of teaching, and when specific guidance is given it should be clear, limited and never allowed to dominate the player's thinking over his focus on the desired musical product.

Learning to listen is the most important skill every musician must develop. It provides the most objective means for creating, directing, and evaluating playing, and its development will ultimately determine how far the player will advance.

V

Developing a Concept of Sound

The primary manner by which children learn is the process we call imitation, which is a pattern of stimulus/response. We learn to speak by listening to the speech of those around us. We receive, assimilate, and, eventually—through a period of trial and error (practice)—reproduce, albeit with our own unique qualities, the language to which we have been exposed. This process is a perfectly natural one that if allowed to develop normally enables us to communicate with those around us. The process is really a cyclical one; we hear sounds, we engage in a process of sorting out appropriate physical responses, and we reproduce sounds.

What is important to note about this cycle is where it begins, with exposure, absorption, assimilation, and, finally, imitation. Another way of stating this is to say that any intended action or behavior must begin with an idea (concept) of the product. We can grasp this pattern of exposure, practice, and final result quite readily when it comes to human speech, but when we begin to teach music we often frustrate the student's development by artificially starting in the middle of the process.

Usually a brass student's acquaintance with playing will begin with rather specific physical instructions concerning embouchure, breathing, vibrating the lips, and holding the instrument. None of these areas are improper for consideration, but they are often dealt with before the young player has any sense of what sort of sound is characteristic of the instrument. In other words, the player has been taught the various means of production without a clear notion of the product.

To attempt to play without a good sense of how one wishes to sound is akin to attempting to learn to speak a language without having heard the language. The principal reason so many young players sound poorly is that most of them have only heard each other. If a child grows up in an environment in which people speak with a particular accent or in a cultural setting where poor grammar is the norm, the child's speech will reflect such influences. Likewise, the quality of the music the young player hears will profoundly affect his development.

The creation of any sound, verbal or musical, starts with an idea of that sound. Unfortunately, young musicians are frequently instructed in physiological matters before ever having heard a single beautiful phrase of music. Uppermost in successful music making is to first hear beautiful playing or singing.

Over the years a few of my colleagues have expressed some reservations about the approach I advocate. One of the questions frequently asked is how a teacher who is not a fine performer on a particular instrument can properly demonstrate fine playing. The question is a valid one deserving an answer. There are at least three ways in which the concept of a beautiful sound may be instilled in a young performer apart from having the teacher demonstrate on the instrument. First, live demonstrations by other fine players may be employed. This is the most desirable means of setting an example if the teacher is unable to play well on the particular instrument. Second, recordings may be utilized. Even students in the most far-flung communities have access in today's technological world to excellent recorded performances. Third, if the teacher is proficient on another instrument, he or she should play for the student on that instrument. It is far better, for example, for a good clarinetist to demonstrate well on that instrument than to play poorly on a brass instrument. Many of the attributes that we attach to a successful sound (fullness, centeredness, warmth, ease of production, good intonation, and flowing line) transfer readily in one's imagination from one instrument to another.

Many years ago I had a friend who was an exceptional flute player. When the famous teacher with whom she studied decided to retire, she asked him to suggest someone with whom she might continue to study. He told her he had already arranged for a famous pianist to take her on as a student. Granted, her skills were at a very high level, but her teacher's primary concern, and the point I wish to make here, is that the principal focus of all music teaching should be on musicianship. We often get so tangled up in the specific complexities of a particular instrument that we make playing more difficult and miss what is really important.

For many years I taught with a trombonist whom I consider to be one of the finest brass teachers of our time. We spent many hours over the course of our years together discussing (sometimes arguing over) pedagogical matters. One of the conclusions we reached was that more often than not our best students came to us from teachers whose principal instrument was different from the student's instrument. We decided that this was because people tend not to "over teach" technical matters relating to instruments on which they do not consider themselves expert. Rather, they tend to emphasize such general qualities as sound, relaxation, breathing, and musical phrasing.

When I began my teaching career I found myself obligated to teach other brass instruments in addition to trumpet. Among my assignments were four young trombone players, all of whom possessed a great deal more detailed information about the trombone than I. My comments to them were confined largely to matters of sound, breathing, and musical interpretation. I rarely spoke about embouchure, mouthpieces, or slide positions, simply because I did not think myself qualified to speak about those things as they pertained to the trombone. With my (supposedly more fortunate) trumpet students, I taught at considerable length those esoteric topics on which I was an alleged expert.

To my surprise and dismay, by the end of the school year my trombone students had made considerably more progress than my trumpet students. I learned quickly that the quantity of information dispensed is not to be confused with the quality of instruction. Students improve most when taught the concepts of good sound, good breathing, and singing lines rather than when given lots of specific technical information about their instruments.

Inherent in the concept of a good sound is the basic guidance one needs to play well. Arnold Jacobs puts it this way: "Think ends, not means." The creation of the product in the mind's ear will guide the various aspects of production until the specific physical behaviors have been found that cause the replication of that sound through the instrument.

This approach does two salutary things. First, it follows the natural learning process described earlier, relying on imitation as the chief means by which human beings acquire skills. Second, it makes the process simpler and more direct. One should develop a concept of sound, think that sound, and allow it to guide every aspect of playing.

Specific listening practices may be employed to facilitate the development of a concept of sound. The most critical task is to get the player thinking musical sounds rather than verbal instructions. For this purpose, there is no better method than to have the student sing as much as possible. Solos, études, and ensemble parts should be sung as well as played on the instrument. Only by having the student sing can we be sure the music is really in the player's mind.

Using a recording device is also a great stimulus to better listening. It is amazing how intently any player, even a seasoned professional, will listen when a recorder is on. Merely having the machine going will virtually guarantee better listening and concentration.

Having students play regularly for each other will also inspire more acute listening. Frequent master class performances, when combined with regular public appearances, raise the player's self-awareness and also make playing for others a more usual, less frightening experience.

Students learn much from one another. A player often finds it easier to recognize a problem in someone else's playing than in his or her own. A comment addressed to one player will often find its way home to someone else.

A frequently expressed concern is when the student should be made aware of the importance of developing a concept of sound. I hope the answer is already apparent, but in case there is any doubt, let me be clear about the need to begin to teach this idea before the player attempts the first note. Just as hearing begins before attempts at speech, so learning to listen must begin before playing.

At some level we are musicians before we are brass players, and musical ideas must precede, permeate, and guide all our activities if we are to be as successful as nature and our talents allow.

VI

Posture

There are two criteria by which posture must be judged in terms of its relationship to musical performance: (1) Does it allow the performer to work in the most comfortable manner commensurate with good performance? and (2) Does it allow for the player's most physically efficient and effective performance?

Several attributes attach in a general way to satisfactory posture. These include an overall sense of relaxation as opposed to tension, the ability to be responsive and adaptable rather than rigid, and a physical sense of being able to produce and control motion or flow rather than being locked in a condition of stasis.

Any posture used in musical performance should enhance alertness, concentration, and artistic and technical flexibility. Good posture should also enhance such nonphysical qualities as confidence, calmness, and the ability to focus. Stage appearance is also improved by good posture.

Many performers encounter physical problems in later years that can be traced to postural causes. The difficulty in treating such problems is that while the immediate cause of adverse conditions in the neck, shoulder, or arms or the inability to achieve good breathing may be attributable to a specific postural condition, the underlying stimulus for the postural defect may have a psychological basis such as fear, lack of confidence, mental fatigue, or professional complacency.

While no attempt will be made here to deal with the many possible psychological causes for structural or muscular problems, it should be noted that these root causes require attention if meaningful, long-term solutions are to be realized. We will instead concern ourselves with those desirable physical habits that young players should cultivate early on in their development in order to ensure longer, more healthful careers.

Perhaps the most important idea in acquiring a generally healthful approach to good posture is that of freedom of motion. Playing any instrument involves the use of muscles; some large, some small. Muscles are engaged in two phases of activity. They contract (active behavior) and they relax (passive behavior). They also require an adequate supply of blood in order to function properly, rejuvenate after use, and remain healthy. The most insidious enemy of proper muscular function is tension.

Unfortunately, both the physical act of performing on a musical instrument and the psychological conditions surrounding musical performance tend to be tension inducing. Awareness of these propensities and of appropriate efforts toward an efficient approach is essential for good performance. Good posture is both a by-product of efficient function and a necessary means toward achieving such efficiency.

For the brass player, good posture is vital if the quality of the player's sound is to develop to the finest level. Sound is air set in vibration when it crosses a membrane (the lips), and the ability to achieve quantity and quality with the air (and hence the sound) will be dramatically enhanced or restricted by the player's posture.

Whether the player is standing or sitting, the spine should be elongated. I suggest to my students that they think of standing as tall as possible without straining. This will lengthen the spine and allow the thorax to expand, the shoulders to hang naturally and without tension, and the abdominal region to expand and contract as needed.

What we are seeking is free, full range of motion in order to move whatever amount of air is needed at whatever degree of velocity is required. When required to breathe in and out vigorously, the player should not have to be preoccupied with thinking about posture. Rather, the posture should be such that it facilitates in the most responsive manner possible whatever the player is trying to do.

Establishing a posture that emphasizes height (space), mobility, and volume of air gives the performer freedom to express musical ideas more easily. Conversely, any posture that increases rigidity or reduces air capacity will inhibit performance.

It is often helpful to ask students to stand or sit as is if they are about to be photographed. Most will respond by lengthening the torso to a more efficient position. Perhaps in this age of technology we should avail our students of the benefits of video photography. Many of us are as unaware of how we really look as we are unaware of how we really sound.

Good posture based on the principles of relaxation, freedom, and range of motion should result not only in immediate improvement in the musical product but over the longer term in performance careers much freer from physically debilitating postural problems.

VII

Breathing

Before considering actual suggestions about improving respiratory habits, certain basic respiratory conditions need to be examined. Essentially, in taking even the simplest breath two extensive groups of muscles are involved, those of inspiration and those of expiration. Each group works best when working unopposed by the opposite set.

It is important to understand the difference between positive muscular effort (in this case inhaling air or blowing it out) and isometric tension, that is, muscle working against muscle. Each of the two complex muscle groups involved in breathing (inhalation and exhalation) works best when allowed to work positively without opposition from the other. What is sometimes referred to as control or support is often really a misplaced attempt to govern the action of one set of muscular responses by setting in action an opposite muscular force. Isometric tension often misleads the wind player because it feels as if one is working very hard and therefore doing something productive. I will have more to say later about evaluating playing by feeling.

What we should be seeking from the breath is neither isometric tension nor a false sense of support but rather motion. Good air is always moving. It is either moving in or it is moving out. If it is static, it is bad air and will almost certainly lead to an increase in tension in the body and constriction in the sound.

We also need to consider for a moment the difference between airflow and compression. Airflow refers to the speed with which the air moves in or out of the body. Compression refers to how much pressure the air stream is under. Certain instruments—for example, the tuba—utilize enormous rates of airflow, but that air is generally under only a low to moderate degree of compression. The oboe and the trumpet in the upper register have much lower flow rates, but such breath frequently attains relatively high levels of compression. Nevertheless, the flow rate should be as high as possible for the pitch frequency and dynamic level sought (in other words, motion of breath). This property of motion in the breath produces a higher degree of efficiency in tone production and results in a warmer, freer quality of sound. Keep in mind that as the player changes registers the flow rate/compression level relationship changes. As the player goes lower the flow rate increases and compression is reduced. The reverse occurs as one ascends.

Let me reiterate one important condition before we get into specific suggestions for improving breathing. This concerns how we best coordinate and direct the physical behavior necessary to any willful creative act, whether playing a brass instrument or swinging a golf club. The portion of the brain that best controls specific neuromuscular responses is that which we call the subconscious mind. The conscious mind conceives the idea. The subconscious mind, which in some ways is the more sophisticated, directs the particular neuromuscular responses necessary to implement whatever skill we wish to perform. In other words, our job is to focus our conscious attention on the product and allow the subconscious to direct the means of production.

Since we learn most skills by a process of imitation, we should follow this same approach in the study of instruments. The stimuli that direct our playing should take the form of musical sounds whenever possible. Elaborate verbal instructions, however seemingly correct, not only violate the premise that good ideas need to be presented in a simple, usable form, but they also do not approach the learning of performance skills with the same natural learning process that we follow when learning to speak, sing, dance, or play a sport.

We do not control muscular behavior as well when we try to think directly of the muscles as when we think of a stimulus that triggers the correct responses. In other words, to produce a certain quality of sound, one must first think that sound. The body only does what the mind tells it to do, and in order to provide the best instructions, it is necessary to think clearly of the product we want. It is the responsibility of our conscious mind to create the sound, and it is the responsibility of the subconscious mind to direct the responses necessary for the recreation of that sound.

Think sound, not feeling, and judge sound, not feeling. Only the sound gives us an objective means of guiding and evaluating our playing. Directing and judging playing by feeling is highly subjective, inaccurate, and misleading. No audience or conductor is interested in how our playing feels, only in how it sounds.

Now let us examine some suggestions for improving respiratory function as it pertains to wind instrument playing. First let us consider the importance of good posture. In Chapter 6, posture was discussed, particularly in its effect on playing efficiency and the long-term health of the player. Breathing, more than any other aspect of playing, benefits or suffers as a direct result of posture. The breathing mechanism only functions effectively when operating from a position of good posture. Yet such a simple but critical matter is often taken for granted. Good posture is absolutely essential for good breathing. Good posture is also easy to achieve; the only hard part is remembering to do it.

After years of reading about approaches to teaching breathing and listening to many players speak about the subject, I have reached the conclusion that the best way to achieve good respiratory habits is not by seeking to acquire an abundance of technical knowledge about the breathing process or somehow to develop the ability to consciously control multifaceted muscular responses, but rather to simply concentrate on making the *sound* of a good breath. By using the vowel sound "OH" or "AH," one can breathe in and out a full, flowing air column that can be readily adjusted to accommodate pitch and dynamic level as is musically appropriate.

Making the proper sound by using these single syllables triggers virtually all the physical responses required for a good breath. These sounds certainly meet our requirements for effectiveness and simplicity. They are easy to remember, easy to produce, and they work!

When dealing with virtually all aspects of playing, it is better to employ general, broad concepts (providing they are correct, of course) than narrow, specific directions. Again, this is an example of concentrating on the ends rather than on the means. By thinking of the sound of a good breath rather than on the mechanical intricacies of respiration, we take and use air more efficiently and effectively. We always play better when we think creatively rather than mechanically.

A good breath has a very distinct sound. It has two specific, easily recognized characteristics: it sounds full, and it sounds free flowing. The syllables "OH" or "AH" can readily be breathed in and blown out to meet these requirements.

A crucial factor in the effectiveness of our breathing is the volume of air we take in. A comfortably full breath makes playing easier and produces a more beautiful sound than a small breath. The ease with which the air is expelled is determined in part by the amount of air we inhale. A voluminous breath is much more freely exhaled.

For purposes of wind playing, the upper one-half to two-thirds of our air supply is expelled most efficiently. If one has a capacity of five liters of air, this gives the player about three liters that can be expelled with considerable efficiency. Below that level the work effort will likely have to be increased to such a degree that the sound may become more labored. Each time we breathe, we should take a full breath, use that breath as freely as possible, and then refill. One might visualize this as a string player would use the bow fully, going from frog to tip whenever possible. Needless to say, few phrases require that we expel all our air, but we should use the breath in as flowing a manner as the music permits.

There are two specific situations relating to the breath that need to be addressed. The first concerns the acoustical setting in which we practice. Frequently players must practice in small, dry acoustical environments such as practice cubicles or bedrooms. Such spaces are much smaller than the spaces where we usually perform, and this usually leads the player to underbreathe and to compress the sound. One must try and imagine the larger space where one will actually be performing and practice accordingly.

The second item relates to one's approach to soft playing. Frequently players interpret soft dynamics as negative, as if a soft passage is really a loud passage held back. What happens in this instance is that a high level of blowing effort is maintained, but isometric tension is employed to restrain the dynamic level. The result is a sound characterized by tightness. This is somewhat like depressing the accelerator of an automobile completely to the floor and controlling the car's speed with the brake. It is much better to blow freely with positive energy at a level appropriate to the pitch and dynamic, striving to maintain a full, free flowing sound at all levels. One should always strive for a sense of blowing, of motion, never for a sense of restraining air.

Good respiratory function is the single most important physical skill every brass player must develop. The successful

approach will be one that emphasizes full, relaxed and flowing
air. By listening for the *sound* of a good breath, one can constantly
monitor and improve one's breathing habits.

VIII

Embouchure

The embouchure is to the brass player as the reed is to the wind player, with two differences being that the vibrating membrane is formed from the brass player's own tissue and that the tissue is somewhat malleable, whereas the reed is a rather fixed resistance. Perhaps an even better analogy might be drawn between singers and brass players, since both use vibrating membranes formed from the player's body.

In any event, the embouchure is that portion of the playing apparatus that serves to turn unresonate air into a vibrating air column. How well the embouchure performs this function will have a major effect on the quality of the musical product.

The embouchure is primarily an instrument of response. It responds chiefly to the air stream that activates it. It also responds to the pressure put upon it by the mouthpiece.

In terms of initiative, the main function of the embouchure is to focus the sound at a certain pitch level. The size of the embouchure's aperture is crucial in this regard, and this function is best developed and controlled by concentrating on the desired pitch/timbre rather than by directing thought toward the aperture itself. Certainly no singer would try to achieve a particular pitch or tone color by attempting to think directly of conscious control of the vocal cords. Likewise the aperture of the embouchure results from thinking the pitch.

One of the most challenging aspects of brass teaching is helping beginning players to find a good embouchure formation with comfortable, workable mouthpiece placement.

While there is some variation among players of different brass instruments as to the most desirable mouthpiece placement, there are certain general qualities and guidelines that are more or less universally agreed upon. (Please see the excellent photographs in Philip Farkas's *The Art of Brass Playing*★ for fine examples of embouchure formation as well as indication that there is variation even among the finest players.)

Virtually all good embouchures have a number of readily identifiable characteristics that include:

1. Reasonably firm corners.
2. A gentle closing of the lips, much as if humming the sound "M."
3. A relaxed and responsive center that can vibrate resonantly.
4. A firm chin, pointed downward in a U or V shape from the corners.
5. Reasonably centered mouthpiece placement from side to side and top to bottom and still allowing for well-defined tendencies for the characteristic sounds associated with each particular instrument.
6. What Mr. Farkas calls the "brass player's face," which is really the proper degree of antagonistic muscular behavior between opposing sets of muscles.
7. An overall sense of gentle firmness necessary to center the pitch and tone quality, to play both very softly and at vigorous volumes and still adapt quickly to varying registers.

★ Philip Farkas, *The Art of Brass Playing*, Wind Music, Inc., Rochester, N.Y., 1962, pp. 26-31.

When instructing a beginning player, I recommend the player hum the sound of the letter "M," making the corners slightly firmer and then practicing a single, simple note in the middle register at a moderate volume on the mouthpiece alone. It is desirable that the student practice the mouthpiece extensively before attempting to play on the instrument.

It must be stressed, however, that students should be carefully instructed in how to take in and blow out a full, free flowing breath before attempting even the first sound on the mouthpiece. Nothing else can so quickly lead to embouchure problems as poor use of the air. Since the embouchure primarily responds to the air, it cannot, by definition, function better than the air that activates it. In my teaching experience, most so-called embouchure problems are really brought on by misuse of the air. For all its seeming complexity, the embouchure is a rather simple entity that, much like a singer's vocal cords, tends to be not so much changed or improved in and of itself but rather improved by changing the energy (i.e., the breath) that activates it. Time spent on improving the air will usually do more to improve the workings of the embouchure than the same amount of time spent directly on the embouchure.

In working on embouchure development there are four general areas of concern. First there is pitch accuracy. The frequency at which the embouchure vibrates determines the pitch produced. Yet it is all too easy to blame the embouchure for missed notes. The embouchure, primarily an instrument of response, reacts to produce the pitch we hear, and the note produced is far more a product of our hearing than we often suspect. The primary responsibility lies with our hearing, and the embouchure simply works off the information it is supplied. The solution has far more to do with ear training than embouchure change, and the best approach is almost always through singing. Only then can we be certain the player is focused on the right product.

A second area of concern that often focuses on the embouchure is that of endurance. Virtually every player I have ever met would like increased stamina. Developing a longer lasting embouchure is not, unfortunately, a matter of some special technique or approach. It is simply a matter of developing good fundamental skills and then extending the amount of time we practice those skills. Increased endurance is not so much a goal as a by-product of efficient work.

The third area of development frequently associated with the embouchure is the upper register. Actually, extending one's upper register is quite simple: not necessarily easy, mind you, but simple. It is really a matter of learning to play a good sound in the middle register and then gradually repeat, gradually extending it. Attention should be directed at maintaining and extending a good sound. Quick fixes, gimmicks, and short cuts to range development can lead to serious embouchure problems and should be eschewed. Healthful muscular development and coordination take time, and patience as well as persistence is required.

The fourth area of concern that greatly relates to embouchure is flexibility. While the embouchure must be firm enough to focus a particular pitch, it also must be adaptable enough to react quickly and accurately to pitch and volume changes. The solution here is the gentle firmness referred to earlier, combined with a sense of responsiveness in both the air stream and the embouchure. An embouchure that is locked in a position of rigidity will have neither the responsiveness to assist in producing a warm sound nor the ability to change pitch and volume with facility.

A well-functioning embouchure has a balance of firmness and relaxation and responds readily to the air column. It focuses the sound well at any dynamic level and still retains the elasticity and mobility to make rapid, sometimes large, sometimes subtle adjustments in all registers.

IX

Articulation

Part I—Single Tonguing

Developing fine articulation on a brass instrument is a matter of knowing first how one wishes the articulation to sound and then systematically developing the precise physical responses necessary to create such sounds.

The best way to develop an idea of good articulation is to listen to as many fine players as possible. One should listen to a wide variety of music employing many different styles of articulation. It is also very important to listen to fine musicians other than brass players in order to hear what kinds of articulation styles are used in other performance mediums. Many ideas can readily be adapted for use on brass instruments.

Keep in mind that articulation for a brass instrumentalist is much like diction for a singer. It is that quality that gives definition or character to the beginning of the tone.

For a brass player the most important physical consideration in achieving good articulation is the breath. Poor tonguing is caused more frequently by inadequacies in the breath than by poor tongue placement. As a muscle, the tongue reacts sympathetically to other muscles. If those muscles involved in respiration are relaxed and functioning efficiently then the tongue is apt to do likewise. By contrast, if the airflow is tight, shallow or labored, the muscle we call the tongue will react similarly.

It must be remembered that the tongue articulates the air stream, and it is virtually impossible for the articulation to sound better than the air stream that is being articulated.

The air column should be full and free flowing at all times. Adjustments are made for dynamics and range, of course, but within the parameters dictated by these two conditions, the aforementioned qualities always apply. The player should strive to acquire a full, relaxed inhalation as a matter of course and then expel that full breath in as free flowing a manner as possible. When the breath is moving freely and is of proper fullness, the job of the tongue in achieving the desired articulation will be much easier.

Many method books for beginning players emphasize staccato articulation rather early in the student's work. This often leads the young player to put more emphasis on stopping the sound than on making and continuing it. Full, melodic playing should be strongly emphasized at first. Only after the young player can produce a sustained musical line should any effort be directed at playing shorter notes. Even then, great attention needs to be directed to how the notes are ended. The problems most frequently encountered in ending the sound are using the tongue to stop the note or closing the airflow by tightening the throat. Both these practices produce highly unmusical sounds. The student should be taught to simply cease blowing. This will need to be done with slower passages at first so that the sounds being produced can be clearly heard. Perhaps a series of half notes and half rests, then quarter notes and quarter rests, and so on, could be employed.

The beginning articulation itself is generally rather easy to develop if a few simple ideas are followed. Emphasis should be placed on the importance of the air. In one sense, all attacks are breath attacks; that is, the sound (tone) is always produced by the breath, not the tongue. The tongue stroke merely articulates (defines or gives character) to the sound.

Many teachers and students spend a great deal of time trying to identify exactly where the tongue should strike in the mouth. Such efforts seem to me to be misplaced. Each player is so unique in physical makeup as to make all but general characterizations about tongue placement futile. Rather, I suggest the emphasis be placed on saying and singing the desired articulation. Once the student can sing the sought after quality of articulation, it is usually a short, easy step to transferring that articulation to the instrument.

The sound *tu* (pronounced "tew") has long been the accepted standard articulation in brass playing. Using the same vowel but altering the initial consonant to produce the sound *du* ("dew") results in a softer, more legato character. Conversely, strengthening the *t* in the *tu* syllable will give a more marked character. The best approach to developing these sounds and their almost infinite variety of shadings is first to sing the desired sound, then to play it on the mouthpiece, and then to play it on the instrument, all the while emphasizing the importance of full, free flowing breath and of mentally singing rather than attempting an analysis by feeling of what the tongue is doing.

Practice on articulated passages should proceed slowly at first, with great importance attached to listening. After the desired sound is achieved, attention may be given to faster articulated passages. It is not at all uncommon, however, to hear fast passages played in a blurred, indistinct manner because of the lack of slow, thoughtful practice.

In the early stages of learning to articulate well, it is vital to develop a sense of rich, resonant singing. Easy, seemingly effortless articulations are best achieved by slower practice that allows the student to really hear what kind of sounds are actually being produced and whether the air, embouchure, tongue, and valves (slide) are well coordinated. The emphasis should always be placed on good listening and good airflow rather than on physical analysis of the minute, particularized behavior of the tongue.

Part II—Multiple Tonguing

Before the young brass player begins to work on double and triple tonguing, there are two areas of playing that must be developed. The first requirement is that the player should have a full, free sound. The second requirement is that the single tongue articulation should be good. Development of fine multiple tonguing is based on these two suppositions, and until they are well established, work in double and triple tonguing should be postponed.

Articulation may be defined as the character or definition that we give to the sound (tone). It is therefore incumbent upon each player to make certain the sound is of a high order. If the player is using a full, rich, and freely blown air column, improving tonguing skills should prove much easier.

When beginning to actually practice multiple tonguing passages, serious attention should continue to be given to the air stream and the sound it is producing. If the air stream is neglected, the quality of the articulation will be compromised.

To practice multiple tonguing, the player should begin with double tonguing and then proceed to triple tonguing. The player is well advised to devote much of the early work on articulation on the mouthpiece alone. It is much easier to evaluate the sounds on the mouthpiece than it is on the instrument.

The basic sound is *tu* ("tew") or *du* ("dew") for more legato passages. This is the normal, garden variety form of articulation used in a myriad of musical circumstances. In multiple tonguing the *ku* ("kew") sound is substituted in various patterns of alternation with the *tu* sound. It is best to practice the usual single tongue syllable first to establish the desired sound, then substituting the downstroke sound *ku* (*gu* for more legato passages), striving to make the substitute sounds match the original as nearly as possible.

I recommend extensive practice on the following patterns. The tone quality should always be full, and notes should be sustained. Avoid short, choppy notes. They quickly lead to tight, guttural sounds. Practice on more staccato work can come much later after the basic technique has been well developed. Remember these patterns should be spoken and sung first, then played on the mouthpiece, and finally played on the instrument.

Double tonguing:

Tu-tu-tu-tu, etc.
Ku-ku-ku-ku, etc.
Tu-ku-tu-ku, etc. (Standard pattern)
Ku-tu-ku-tu, etc.

Triple tonguing:

Tu-tu-tu, etc.
Ku-ku-ku, etc.
Tu-tu-ku, etc. (Standard pattern)
Tu-ku-tu, etc. (Standard pattern)
Ku-tu-tu, etc.
Ku-tu-ku, etc.

Many players are concerned about acquiring speed in multiple tonguing much too early in the process. Sound, evenness, and clarity all are more important than speed in the early stages of development.

Good articulation, like clear articulate speech, needs time to develop. Any attempts at short cuts are likely to produce unsatisfactory results that ultimately will result in a poorer product and possible long-lasting problems. Fine breathing, constant attention to producing a fine musical sound and line, and careful, steady work will ensure the most satisfactory progress.

X

Mouthpiece Playing

Mouthpiece practice is strongly recommended for students of all brass instruments from the very beginning of study. In fact, students will benefit enormously from practice on the mouthpiece alone before attempting to play on their instruments.

There are several compelling reasons for mouthpiece practice. First, such practice is simpler than playing the instrument. The instrument presents enough additional factors to become a distraction from the most fundamental act of producing a sound. Practicing on the mouthpiece alone emphasizes the fact that the player is the real source of the sound.

Second, it is easier to identify those areas that need work. If, for example, the student is not playing with a full, rich column of air, this deficiency will be noticed more readily than when playing on the instrument. As with any desirable change, the most important stage in correcting a problem is awareness of the need for improvement. Playing on the mouthpiece dramatically demonstrates this need.

Third, mouthpiece practice has a markedly positive effect on the student's listening skills. Because there are no valves or slide to help in pitch placement, the entire responsibility for pitch accuracy must be met by the player. Students who tend to play out of tune on the instrument often show marked improvement after playing the same phrase only a few times on the mouthpiece. The instrument is used, quite wrongly, as a crutch enabling the student to play approximately the right pitch. In reality, the quality of the pitch can be no better than that which the player produces. Removing the instrument lays bare the player's responsibility.

Fourth, any misuse of the embouchure in terms of placement, response, excessive tension, or mouthpiece pressure will become immediately more apparent to the player when the instrument is not present to distract from the source of the problem. Awareness of such problems is absolutely necessary to their solution.

Players at all levels can benefit from thoughtful, ongoing mouthpiece practice. Such efforts do not have to be terribly time consuming, but they should be a daily part of every player's routine.

For the beginning student, mouthpiece playing need take only a few minutes of the practice day. Additional time is advised, however. The player should start in a comfortable middle range where the sound is easy to produce.

Learning to play very simple lines with a good sound, good embouchure formation and mouthpiece placement may take a little time, but it is vital that the student start properly. As soon as a good foundation has been set the young player should start to expand his or her efforts, moving progressively from simple phrases to longer, more musically complex lines. The idea should always be one of beautiful singing, not of buzzing notes.

Range, articulation, and slurring all respond well to mouthpiece practice. Etudes, solos, and orchestral excerpts benefit greatly from being practiced on the mouthpiece. While such practice is not as musically satisfying as playing the instrument and should not be thought of as taking the place of such practice, it can be a most efficient means of getting to a final product of higher quality more quickly. Mouthpiece practice virtually always results in easier, more accurate and healthful playing.

Advanced players who often work several hours a day can easily incorporate ten or fifteen minutes of mouthpiece work into a daily routine. Because the time spent on good mouthpiece practice increases the likelihood the player will produce the sound more efficiently, a frequent result is considerably improved endurance.

XI

The Warm-Up

Most brass players agree on the need to perform a daily warm-up. There appears to be, however, less agreement on the exact purpose of such a warm-up or on the form that it should take. One point of view stresses the physical need to warm up the muscular tissue involved in performance. Another idea suggests the importance of the psychological security resulting from a thorough routine.

For a better understanding of just what a warm-up routine can and cannot (or perhaps, should or should not) do, several points need to be made preparatory to outlining a specific set of procedures.

The most important purpose of warming up is to formulate and connect the most appropriate musical concepts with the most efficient physical responses. The reason one plays is to make music, and the process of musical creativity must begin at the very outset of one's practice.

The supply of blood (and hence, oxygen) to the lips is among the most generous of any part of the human body (only the brain regularly receives a greater supply). So, to warm up the lips in the athletic sense of stimulating increased blood flow to a joint or muscle is unnecessary. It is already done. What does need to happen, however, is for the player's mind to formulate the finest artistic stimuli (sounds) possible. The formulation of these sounds, followed by their implementation on the instrument, is the key to creative success.

Such a musical process also serves the very real psychological need to know that one's responses and technical abilities are all functioning well. By concentrating on the sound one wants, the process becomes one of controlling response by controlling the stimulus, rather than the pseudoscientific approach of trying to control muscles by direct, conscious thought. To try to alter responses of such muscle systems as are found in the embouchure, abdominal, thoracic, and diaphragmatic regions by attempting to think of them directly is to frustrate the most efficient use of these systems and to create great psychological insecurity at the same time. In other words, think the sounds one wishes to produce. The appropriate physical responses will follow in due course.

This approach, if followed from the outset, will produce not only a highly satisfactory warm-up routine but also a method for practicing and performing that sets the highest standards for efficiency and productivity.

Several guidelines must be strictly adhered to in any warm-up routine if such a routine is to be really successful. These principles are as follows:

1. All practice must be of the highest musical quality. Technical accomplishments apart from musical goals have no value whatsoever.
2. A good warm-up routine must be comprehensive without being excessive in length.
3. The player should vary the routine each day in order to keep the playing interesting. Mindless repetition is potentially harmful.
4. The player should not become so dependent on a warm-up routine that he cannot function if he does not have time to warm up. Circumstances sometimes

prohibit warming up, and the player should be capable of playing anytime and under almost any circumstances. Mental flexibility and adaptability are as important as technical training.

The warm-up routine that I employ incorporates these ideas and is divided into several stages, each of which is based on the successful completion of the preceding phase. The routine I am going to suggest should be thought of as a broad outline, not a rigidly prescribed set of steps. Each player must adapt by expanding, reducing, or modifying the routine to suit the individual's needs. Again, great care must be taken to vary the exact material each day so that the playing stays fresh and thoughtful. It is best to have a number of studies in each area that will accomplish essentially the same ends. These may then be interchanged on a rotating basis.

The length of work in each section should also be varied occasionally to prevent over dependence on exact repetition. My warm-up routine varies in length from five minutes to half-an-hour, depending on how much time I have, the playing conditions I will encounter that day, and the problems I may be experiencing at a given time.

The general categories into which I divide my warm-up follow.

1. Breathing

The breath is the fuel that makes musical vibrations possible. As such, its proper use is essential for good playing. Far too much detailed and technical information has been written about "how" to breathe. Rather than thinking of the physiology of respiration, the player is generally better served by thinking of the sound of a full, relaxed breath (the word "OH" seems to work well) and by concentrating on making that sound when inhaling and exhaling rather than worrying about what some obscure muscle is or is not doing. If the breath makes a full, free flowing "OH" sound, the breath is satisfactory. Practice breathing in and out in such a fashion until the procedure is comfortable and well assimilated.

2. Mouthpiece Playing

Practice musical tunes on the mouthpiece. Avoid long, boring exercises. Make music immediately! Cover all the ranges, various articulations, and dynamics in the first few minutes. At first, this will seem a bit reckless, but the player will soon discover that achieving the correct responses depends on thinking good musical sounds, not thinking about controlling specific muscles. Make the mouthpiece practice as musically interesting as possible. Play études, solos, and excerpts as well as simple tunes. Mouthpiece playing is an extremely efficient form of practice and should occupy a sizable portion of the warm-up routine. Ten to fifteen minutes of mouthpiece practice are desirable.

3. Lyrical Studies

Next comes the first practice on the instrument. Slow, lyrical melodies are useful in the beginning. Works such as Vincent Cichowicz's *Flow Studies*, James Stamp's *Warm-ups* or Emory Remington's *Trombone Warm-ups* are good, but they must be played musically rather than as exercises. Following these studies should come melodies of a somewhat faster nature. Herbert L. Clarke's *Technical Studies for Cornet*, for example, are wonderfully helpful if played for their melodic value.

By the completion of this section, the player should be ready to encounter the day's playing demands. Remember, however, that the warm-up routine must serve, not enslave, the player. It must be done thoughtfully, flexibly, and, above all, musically if it is to be of greatest value.

Remember that it is equally important to warm up well and also to be able to play without warming up when necessary. With practice and concentration one can *will* oneself to be warmed up when absolutely necessary.

XII

Slurring

Slurring, or lip slurs as they are often called among brass players, is the art of connecting two or more notes of different pitch as completely and fluidly as possible. In reality a slur is the absence of any audible interference between two notes. The two notes are connected in what to the ear sounds like a seamless line. Whether the notes are only a half step apart or many notes away from one another, a smooth, unbroken connection is the objective.

Every note played on every type of instrument has a specific acoustical property that must be achieved with proper pitch and timbre. Yet the greater problem for many players is not creating the individual notes so much as connecting those notes into a musically meaningful phrase. Notes can only be connected two basic ways, by slurring or with articulation.

What is imperative for brass players is to keep uppermost the concept of continuous wind moving through the phrase, whether slurring or articulating. (Clearly, I am not referring to detached notes, a separate musical issue with its own aesthetic challenges.)

One might consider a slur as a *glissando* speeded up so that the notes between the two pitches are not actually heard by the listener. In other words, the air/sound are continuous.

With young brass players, one of the most effective approaches to teaching good slurring is to have the student play *glissandi* slowly on the mouthpiece, achieving something of the effect of a siren. This process insures an unbroken continuation of the sound, including all the pitches between the two desired notes. With time, the slur can be speeded up so that the inner notes are inaudible but without losing the connected quality between the principal notes. Unfortunately, the usual alternative is a slight but disruptive break between the two notes. While not actually an authentic articulation, the resultant break is as disruptive as articulating the second note.

It is also helpful to think a common vowel sound for the two notes, regardless of the pitch ("OH–OH"). The old approach of thinking vowel sound change ("OH–EE," or the reverse for a downward slur) results in change in timbre and an overly mechanical sound.

Good slurs are created with a thick, continuous air stream and not with deliberate mechanical constrictions. In fact, a fine slur should have as one of its distinctive qualities a decidedly unmechanical smoothness. Any change in embouchure should be efficiently minimal, and muscular contractions in the throat should be nonexistent. Good slurs should be seamless.

This approach will take time and will require patience on the part of the player, but ultimately the musical product will be of a flowing, aesthetically pleasing character.

XIII

Intonation

Few tasks of the brass player are more constant or demanding than the requirement to play well in tune. To play with good intonation, several skills must be highly developed.

Paramount is the ability to listen critically and objectively. Listening is the primary skill for all musicians, and in no other area of performance does it play a more indispensable role than in achieving good intonation. I refer the reader to the earlier chapter on developing listening skills for more detailed comments on this critical requirement.

Of similar importance to listening skills are well-developed mechanical skills, the most important of which are good use of the air and of the embouchure (both discussed in some detail earlier). The combination of critically perceptive listening with fluid, efficient mechanical responses is absolutely essential to playing well in tune. While obvious, such requirements can hardly be overemphasized.

It is interesting to note that performers with really beautiful sounds almost always play well in tune, while players with poor sounds rarely play well in tune.

One of the most effective means of creating awareness of both pitch accuracy and tone quality is to have the player perform a passage on the mouthpiece. Mouthpiece playing is really a kind of *solfège* for the brass player in that any mechanical aid from the instrument is eliminated, and the player is entirely responsible for the product. The ensuing awareness almost inevitably leads to rapid, substantial improvement.

To play with good intonation, the player must know the characteristics of his or her instrument. While modern brass instrument and mouthpiece makers have made great strides in equipment design, the player is ultimately responsible for the final degree of excellence in tuning. Playing circumstances change constantly, and the player can never abdicate responsibility for the quality of the tuning.

Each player should be intimately familiar with the tuning characteristics of his equipment. Young players in particular should make use of a tuner to check the vagaries of their instruments, at the same time remembering that using a tuner is only a beginning guide that must be supplemented with continuous, sophisticated listening.

The mouthpiece of a brass instrument can have a decidedly important effect on intonation. The student is wise to seek guidance from an expert teacher in choosing such a critical piece of equipment. When a mouthpiece and instrument are well suited to one another and to the player, there is a noticeable improvement in intonation as well as in ease of production, articulation, and general facility. Never, however, should the player think even for an instant that equipment is a substitute for finely developed playing skills or that good equipment relieves the player of final responsibility.

The medium with which one plays has a profound impact on tuning. The modern piano, a rather ubiquitous form of accompaniment, is inflexible in its even-tempered scale, and many players find tuning with a piano to be a real challenge. The piano is out of tune with itself in the strictest acoustical sense, and, of course, it is completely uncompromising, so the instrumentalist must make all the adjustments.

Generally the same challenges apply to tuning with an organ, except that organ pipes range drastically in length and respond to changes in room temperature at vastly different speeds depending upon their size. This sometimes presents the instrumentalist with the problem of just which portion of the organ's scale to match, since the organ may not be completely in tune throughout its entire range. The only solution (and it is less than satisfactory) is for the brass player to continue to listen and adjust as well as possible. (This problem does not exist with those otherwise unfortunate abominations known as electronic "organs.")

Playing with an instrumental ensemble presents a multitude of intonation challenges. Strings, woodwinds, and brasses all respond to changes in temperature or humidity. Even the personalities of the players and their willingness to compromise and cooperate enter into the outcome. Playing in a section requires considerable personal as well as musical skill if the final product is to be truly excellent, and the most creditable players are those who put the quality of the musical product ahead of personal positions.

A serious factor in brass intonation involves the use of mutes. While it is impossible to generalize in a way that accurately covers all the possibilities for intonation variations among the different types of mutes, it is correct to say that straight mutes and Harmon mutes tend to varying degrees of sharpness, while cup mutes are inclined toward lowering the pitch. As suggested earlier, working with a tuner can give a clearer indication of the direction and extent of pitch problems.

Playing well in tune is a never-ending challenge for even the most experienced player. A combination of good listening, excellent production, and awareness of changing conditions can take every player a long way toward playing well in tune.

XIV

The Upper Register

More and more, players are pursuing ever higher goals in terms of range development. In and of itself the pursuit of such increased accomplishment is a worthy task, but many young players expend great amounts of time, effort, and money seeking such achievements by unproductive and sometimes harmful means.

We will first examine just what it is that constitutes an artistically acceptable upper register, and then we will consider ways that may prove most effective in obtaining this sometimes difficult objective.

The first and most important characteristic of the high register is exactly the same as any other part of the playing range; it must be musical. All other requirements are secondary to this one, and, in fact, regardless of what other technical skills may be acquired, without genuine musicality, all else counts for little. Fortunately, the stringent requirement that the upper register be musical is actually a helpful demand, as we will learn a bit later.

A fine high register must sing. No other quality of playing is quite so important as the ability to spin out a beautiful, lyrical, flowing line. One must be able to play high at various dynamic levels, with good articulation, proper use of vibrato, and good intonation. What is not acceptable and is too often settled for, is merely hitting the notes. Such a limited objective has no artistic value.

Perhaps the best way to go about developing the upper register is to listen to fine performers, and I do not mean just brass players. Rather, listen to other musicians as well, especially to fine singers. There is a regrettable tendency among many instrumentalists to try to reduce every musical accomplishment to a narrow, quantifiable muscular calculation. Therefore, one must be especially careful when listening to other brass players to listen for musical as well as technical values. There is less danger of such narrow listening if one listens to a performance medium other than one's own.

Certainly the mechanical functions necessary to good upper register playing are not to be overlooked—rather, the opposite. They become ever more critical with the added difficulty of increased range. It therefore becomes even more imperative that we seek those approaches that make such difficulties more manageable.

A genuinely musical approach will serve our needs more satisfactorily than a program limited to specific mechanical accomplishments. It is necessary to remember that a player is a total unit, and that the whole of playing is better served by a valid, comprehensive concept than by trying to think consciously of the individual parts involved in playing.

First, let us consider basic sound production. The two most important physical elements in sound production are the air stream and the embouchure. Both have been much written about and discussed. Suffice it to say here that good sound production depends on a voluminous, free flowing column of air setting in vibration a responsive, well-formed embouchure.

What has not been adequately written about is the source of direction and motivation for the activities of these two essential elements. The best source of direction for both is identical: the sound in the player's mind. No aspect of playing is exempt from the control of the mind, either at a conscious or subconscious level. This is as true of breath and embouchure as it is of speaking, writing, or any other activity. The critical point to grasp is that all these activities are responses to stimuli and that it is the stimuli that govern the responses. It then follows logically that the way to alter (improve) responses is to alter stimuli. Thinking of the means (muscular contraction) by which a response is made is much less efficient than thinking of the end result (concept) to which those means are applied.

For example, rather than thinking of "how" to take a full breath, think the sound of a full breath and imitate that sound. Muscle systems respond far better to conceptual stimuli than to attempts at direct control.

In working to develop the upper register the player must first, then, have a basic approach to playing that is sound oriented rather than muscularly or analytically oriented. Such an approach must be thoroughly developed in the middle register before extended attempts are made at playing higher. The sound must be full, rich, and flowing. Lines must sing beautifully and intonation must be secure. Then, and only then, should the gradual extension of the upper register be undertaken.

An excellent way to approach higher playing is on the mouthpiece. It is actually helpful in many instances if the player is unaware of the specific pitch being played. I have had numerous students who were so afraid of playing high that they got tighter and tighter as they ascended, but who, when asked to play only on the mouthpiece and were therefore not aware of how high they were actually playing, were able to continue upward for several additional steps.

It is especially important for the player seeking to enhance high playing not to set goals that are unrealistic. The time frame for adding range requires patience and perseverance. Good usable additions to the high range need slow, systematic acquisition and practice for dependability.

It is much better to practice material that is musical in nature rather than dry exercises designed only to build muscular strength. The problem of high playing is not nearly so much a matter of strength as it is one of achieving the proper balance between good airflow and compression. Errors almost always occur on the side of excessive compression, thereby shutting down the airflow to the embouchure.

Regular amounts of practice devoted to deep, vigorous inhalation and exhalation will produce better results than conscious attempts at increased muscular contraction. By thinking of large, free flowing quantities of air, the player is less likely to shut off the airflow with the throat or the tongue. One should strive for the richest sound possible in the high range. The air column should be thick and fast moving. Large quantities of air serve the embouchure better than a narrow, highly compressed air stream.

In closing, let me repeat the three most important facets of practice necessary to develop high register playing. These requirements should be uppermost in the player's mind. First, the playing should always be as musical as possible. Second, adequate time must be allowed for the upper register to develop. Be patient. Third, a good upper register is merely the extension of those skills required in good middle register playing.

There are no tricks, gimmicks, or shortcuts to upper register playing. No exotic technical feats, special equipment, or method books can give one a genuinely good high range. Only continuous, musically sensible practice provides an ultimate answer.

XV

Endurance

Endurance for a brass player comes as a result of fine playing skills, extensive practice, and excellent concentration. There really are no secret formulae for endurance. No special equipment or physical tricks can achieve the same accomplishments as proper preparation.

Perhaps endurance is better thought of as a by-product rather than as a specific objective. If one concentrates on a fine sound and on good breathing habits, the results are not only better sound and technique but also added endurance. Thinking directly about endurance will not cause more efficient playing, and, in fact, focusing on the problem rather than the solutions exacerbates the problem.

The finest technical skills are necessary to play at the highest levels of quality and with good endurance. By focusing on outstanding musical goals, one plays most efficiently, and such efficiency produces better endurance. Worrying about endurance is likely to induce paranoia and cause poor production.

In order for endurance to develop, three areas mentioned earlier must be cultivated. Having in one's mental ear a beautiful, musical sound is the greatest and necessarily the first requirement. All other demands, breathing, embouchure, articulation, and intonation will be guided and developed by this concept of sound. The player should be constantly trying to improve on this concept, and as a result, to demand of himself or herself better breathing, better embouchure function, and so forth in order to produce this higher musical product. Such advances in the excellence and efficiency of skills should continue for as long as one plays.

These skills must not only be practiced well but extensively and continually. While muscle memory is rather long (one never really loses the ability to ride a bicycle or swing a baseball bat), muscle endurance can only be maintained by regular use. Practicing must be done in a way to meet specific playing demands. If one practices well but only once a week, one should not expect to have significant stamina. Daily work is essential.

That having been said, the quality and quantity of practice are both vitally important. Just as fine practice done infrequently produces poor endurance, so does inefficient practice done extensively. Poor, inefficient playing does little for either musicianship or endurance.

Here is where the third quality, concentration, is vital. The ability to focus on the task at hand and to call up one's well practiced abilities on demand is the key not only to improved endurance but to overall good playing.

Most of the playing problems that are often misdiagnosed as lack of endurance are really caused by poor concentration that leads to poor, inefficient production. There is a simple way to demonstrate this. The next time a player seems fatigued, have him or her rest for less than a minute (not nearly enough time for real muscular regeneration) and while resting from playing take several full, flowing breaths. Then have the player perform an opening line or two from any of the standard warm-up routine, making certain to play with a full, singing breath. Then immediately return and play the line that previously sounded poor due to what was thought to be fatigue. The results should be enlightening.

It seems to be part of the human condition that one's mind tires along with one's body as one practices. When this occurs a reduction in playing efficiency is inevitable. Frequent breaks are necessary, not just for physical rest but also to allow one's concentration to be restored. Some research suggests that practice breaks should be taken at least every half hour or so.

Finally, focusing one's attention on the music rather than on oneself will result in far more artistic and physically efficient responses, which in turn produce far greater stamina.

XVI

Vibrato

Vibrato can be a wonderful aesthetic addition to a musical sound when applied in a tasteful, appropriate manner. Personal tastes vary, and there are several different ways of producing vibrato on most brass instruments. A number of principles may be applied, however, to almost any musical situation for which vibrato is appropriate.

The vibrato should seem natural and well suited to the overall style of the piece. Vibrato should be such an integral part of the sound that it does not draw attention to itself. Vibrato should neither damage the pitch center nor be relied upon to mask or correct poor pitch.

A good sound should be well focused, and vibrato should enhance rather than damage this centered quality. Any vibrato that draws attention to itself is in some way flawed. Width, speed, and intensity of vibrato are aesthetic choices, influenced by the traditions associated with particular instruments, by personal preferences, and by national or regional styles. A style that is considered aesthetically pleasing in one situation may be unacceptable elsewhere.

The best guide for players concerned about vibrato is to listen to as many fine performers as possible. It is helpful to listen to players from different media and traditions as well as one's own.

Particular pieces require particular styles of vibrato. (In some instances, this means no vibrato.) Certain national styles have long been established in musical circles, and the erudite performer must not only be aware of such considerations but also be able to incorporate them into performances.

Young players often become aware of vibrato early in their development, but they are sometimes at a loss as to how to best produce satisfactory vibrato. Brass players have traditionally employed three ways to produce vibrato. Not all of these forms are equally applicable to all brass instruments, and the terminology describing their production may be confusing.

These categories are hand vibrato (and its distant counterpart, slide vibrato), lip/chin/jaw vibrato, and so-called diaphragmatic vibrato, which is really a pulsating of the breath.

Each player, preferably under the guidance of a fine teacher, must find that type of vibrato most suited to him and his instrument. I have heard each of these forms used successfully (only rarely, however, in the case of diaphragmatic vibrato), and each decision must be carefully made on a case by case basis.

Complete control—including the ability to use no vibrato—and a highly developed sense of what is aesthetically tasteful in every musical situation are essential. Critical listening and thoughtful practice will combine to enable the player to employ vibrato with skill and appropriateness.

XVII

Braces

Certainly almost everyone who teaches brass instruments has had the experience of having a promising young student walk in for a lesson wearing a new (and often unannounced) set of orthodontic appliances. For many of us (not to mention the student), the frustrations and uncertainties that follow are often many and severe.

First, let me make several observations based on my experience with a number of young players over the years and then suggest an approach to dealing with braces that seems to be satisfactory in most situations.

Most students are nervous and self-conscious about braces, and the teacher should do nothing to add to this psychological discomfort. Even more critical may be the physical discomfort the student is experiencing, and this may be further compounded when an attempt is made to play the instrument.

In a few drastic cases, the student may actually need to discontinue playing during the period the appliances are to be worn. While such an extreme measure is not usually desirable or necessary, the time spent away from the instrument need not result in a total lack of musical growth. In such unfortunate cases, the student should be encouraged to pursue piano studies, sing in a choir, or find other worthwhile avenues for musical growth.

More realistically, the student will probably be able to continue playing, although with various aspects of performance suffering some temporary reduction in quality. Range, endurance, and tone quality seem to be most frequently and severely affected. Such setbacks are often temporary and usually offer no serious, permanent threat to continued progress.

The teacher should carefully monitor the student's work, making certain no abnormalities are developing and watching for any signs of discomfort that cause physical distortion. The teacher should also be willing to accept a slower rate of progress if the braces hinder development. By emphasizing such aspects as reading, rhythm, and key study, the student may continue to develop as a musician while postponing certain physical aspects of development until later.

The most critical and potentially dangerous time for the student with braces occurs when the braces are removed. My observations indicate that this is when most serious problems occur. If for no other reason, problems at this stage should be carefully considered because, unlike those problems that may have arisen when braces were put on, any difficulties which develop now have more potential for permanence.

Excessive pressure, unusual mouthpiece placement, early fatigue, embouchure distortion, spread, unfocused tone qualities, and severe loss of range are among the most commonly observed characteristics. While none of these is an unusual occurrence, the onset of such problems can be a real source of concern to the player. All too often the player suddenly regresses to a much lower level of playing than he or she enjoyed just prior to the removal of braces.

Perhaps the greatest difficulty the young player faces in dealing with all the different physical feelings in going from playing with braces to playing without them is the sense of conflicting and confusing neurological signals. What should have been a happy return to normalcy often becomes a depressing, frustrating experience.

After trying a number of approaches to dealing with the removal of braces, the following procedure seems to offer the best likelihood of success. I have tried this process with a number of young players, and it seems far more satisfactory than more traditional approaches.

The plan involves a considerable amount of cooperation among the student, the instrumental music teacher, the parents, and the orthodontist. It is based on the simple premise that the student should make a fresh start on the instrument under the careful supervision of a well-qualified teacher.

There are three very important stages in making the adjustment to playing without braces. The first step is that as soon as the braces are removed the student should discontinue playing for an extended period of time. A minimum of two weeks is recommended. A month or six-week period is even more desirable. This is most practically done over summer vacation or perhaps Christmas break, when the student has no performance responsibilities, and, of course, it requires coordination and cooperation with the orthodontist and the music teacher. The reason for this deliberate hiatus is to give the student's neurological system time to forget how things "felt" when playing with braces. Upon returning to practice after the designated time off, the player will only have to deal with new signals rather than the conflict between old and new. This reduces the frustration level of the player. The student must abide by the agreement—absolutely no playing during this time. Do not even put the mouthpiece to the face.

The second stage occurs when the agreed-upon date arrives for starting to play again. The student should visit the teacher daily for at least a week, during which time work is done on proper breathing habits and on simple mouthpiece playing, making sure that mouthpiece placement and embouchure are good. Each lesson need only last a few minutes, and the first few days the student is not allowed to play except in lessons. As work progresses, the student may practice at home for limited but gradually increasing amounts of time.

If progress is satisfactory, it is then possible to move to the third stage of the program. Begin by playing simple melodic material, always striving for free, voluminous breathing, a good sound, and acceptable embouchure formation and mouthpiece placement. Gradually, and I emphasize gradually, the student may progress to more demanding material. It is vital that the student's development not be rushed. Good playing habits must not only be taught and learned initially, they must be allowed time to become an integral and dependable part of the student's approach to the instrument. No aspect of development should be hurried. The area the student will most likely attempt to rush is range development. Progress must be carefully monitored and the range allowed to grow at a gradual, healthful rate. Few areas hold potential for greater damage than premature attempts at the upper register.

The program described takes time, thought, and patience on the part of all concerned. We have all seen the frustrations if students proceed directly from playing with braces to playing without braces. Often the results have been dismal. This slower, carefully planned, and supervised transition has proven much more satisfactory.

XVIII

Teaching the Young Orchestral Player

Several years ago I had the experience of assisting a young high school age player who had been selected for his all-state orchestra and who found himself having to play the high trumpet part (piccolo D) in Ravel's *Bolero*. The young man was a capable player with a good background for someone of his age. He was not, however, prepared by experience, development, or even equipment to play this particular part. The real solution to his problem was not in finding some last-minute means of helping him get through such a difficult part, but rather in the conductor choosing music that is appropriate for the stage of development for the players involved.

Orchestral parts that appear to be quite simple can be impossibly difficult. Sometimes there is little correlation between the difficulty of the string parts and the wind parts, so that selecting repertory that is appropriate for the playing skills of the entire ensemble is extremely challenging.

There are three problems pertaining to young orchestral brass players that must be addressed if satisfactory development and performance is to ensue. First is that of transposition and clef reading. It has been the practice of composers throughout the centuries to write parts according to the prevailing customs of the times. These conventions of orchestration have sometimes been done for the most practical of reasons and sometimes merely out of custom. Nevertheless, the orchestral player must deal with transposition and clefs from day one. So the young brass player should start working on transposition or clef reading as soon as other fundamentals such as breathing, rhythm, and moderate range development have been accomplished.

Early practice should be very simple. Easy melodic material should be used first, long before work is done on actual orchestral excerpts. Two of my favorite books for trumpet, for example, are the *First Book of Practical Studies* and the *Second Book of Practical Studies* by Robert Getchell.* These simple melodic studies afford ample opportunity to work on transposition in the context of very basic musical lines. The overwhelming likelihood is that the student is playing a B-flat trumpet or B-flat cornet. Comparable material should be employed for the other instruments.

Gradually more difficult material may be introduced until the student is ready to work on actual orchestral passages. Numerous orchestral excerpt books are readily available, and in many instances complete parts are available. Of paramount importance, however, is the sense of how good orchestral playing sounds, and to learn this, the young player should hear live performances by professional players and study recordings regularly.

The second major challenge facing the young orchestral player is dealing with the wide array of technical demands made by the orchestral repertory. The player may find himself playing a rather simple, straightforward part in an eighteenth-century overture on one part of the program and perhaps something as high and technically demanding as the aforementioned *Bolero* later on in the program.

---

* Robert W. Getchell, *First Book of Practical Studies*, Belwin, N.Y., 1955; Robert W. Getchell, *Second Book of Practical Studies*, Belwin, N.Y., 1955.

Young players today are often more sophisticated in their knowledge of orchestral playing and in the equipment they own than was the case only a few decades ago. It is not unheard of that a really serious high-school age trumpeter will not only possess a B-flat trumpet, but perhaps also a C, a D-E-flat, and a piccolo trumpet. While such equipment, if skillfully employed, can make the player's task easier and more musically satisfying, it may be a mistake to suggest a student play a particular part on C trumpet just because the part is notated for C trumpet. The choice of a certain instrument is frequently dictated by a number of conditions that may not be immediately obvious to a nontrumpet playing conductor. In such cases the teacher/conductor should have the student consult an experienced brass player whenever possible. The piccolo D part in *Bolero*, for example, is played much less often today on a D trumpet than on a piccolo G or piccolo A.

I have frequently heard young players attempt to perform Handel's *Messiah* on a B-flat trumpet. The results, lamentably, are usually less than optimal.

The player should be strongly advised, however, that one does not simply pick up a C trumpet (or descant horn, alto trombone, or F tuba) and play it with no problems. Each instrument is unique, and adequate time must be allowed for even the most rudimentary acquaintance. As a general rule, the quality of intonation inherent in the instrument deteriorates as the instruments go from larger to smaller.

The best approach is to acquire a well-developed playing style on one's regular instrument and then proceed systematically to the more exotic instruments. Such an approach takes time; years, not days or weeks.

The final major concern facing the aspiring orchestral player concerns style. Orchestral style covers a wide range of areas including, but not limited to, tone color, articulation, volume, and vibrato. Furthermore, great variety must be developed within each of these areas in order to do justice to the varied musical situations one encounters. The tone color suitable for a Mozart overture is noticeably different from what one would expect in a composition by Gershwin. Articulation in a Brahms symphony is radically different from that which is appropriate in certain passages by Stravinsky.

The possibilities are infinite, and anyone seeking a clear, simple set of rules will be disappointed. Orchestral playing styles vary considerably from country to country and from orchestra to orchestra. The student should, by attending fine concerts whenever possible and by listening extensively to recordings, absorb as many different ideas and approaches as possible.

XIX

Preparation:
Solo, Chamber, and
Large Ensemble Playing

Solo Playing

Most players have clear recollections of their early solo performances. The experience for many was a watershed experience, and the outcome may have had a profound and lasting influence on the young performer.

It is important to the young player's development that the early experience in solo playing be positive. Poor experiences tend to burden the performer with a long-lasting lack of self-confidence. If the effort is rewarding and the product satisfactory, the student may be inspired to greater efforts in the future. All too often the result is one of frustration, disappointment, and even embarrassment.

I have serious reservations about solo contests in which aspiring young performers receive letter or number grades supported only by cursory comments. Each student progresses at an individual rate, and the unique opportunity to teach each student according to that student's needs and talents is lost by the requirement that each person's playing be categorized. Learning curves vary widely for different individuals, and a student who worked hard but received a low score at a certain stage of maturity may be dissuaded from continued effort. That same student, with the proper individual attention and patience, may blossom at another time.

Solo material and performances should be planned to encourage students as well as to challenge them. It is better to give a student a real chance to enjoy a successful performance experience than to challenge the player with a piece so difficult that he or she has only a marginal chance of playing well. Whether working with a beginner or an advanced player, the teacher's task is to find literature that helps the student advance musically, technically, and in self-confidence. Some teachers assign material well beyond the student's current ability in the hope that the student will rise to such an extreme challenge. Frustration and even physical damage may result. Genuine progress is sometimes slow and needs to be pursued with intelligence and patience. A solo should be chosen with the appropriate musical and pedagogical considerations in mind.

After a player has advanced to the level of playing a recital, the number of considerations that must be taken into account rises significantly. Students are often so eager to play that they choose programs beyond their abilities. The teacher must guide the student toward a realistic, playable program.

When programming a recital, it is wise to include a considerable amount of material that one has performed before. Most players only come to feel that they know a piece well after they have played it in public several times. Programming an entire recital of pieces that one is playing in public for the first time is extremely risky. It is best to work new material into one's repertory one or two pieces at a time. This will allow for continued growth in repertory while maintaining a sense of security and confidence.

Some players are so eager to perform that they construct recitals that are far too long. Everyone has a finite amount of endurance (even the audience). Make certain the player has the physical stamina to actually play the material. A program that is workable in rehearsal becomes more challenging in public performance. As a general guideline, a performer should be able to play through a program two or three times in immediate succession in rehearsal in order to have enough endurance to perform it once in public.

Players often choose music that is clearly too hard for them. While it is laudable to undertake challenges and risks, there must be a strong element of realism. Here the teacher's experience should be firmly exercised.

The program should also be constructed with the audience in mind. There should be balance, and the overall length and choice of material should be suited to the level of musical sophistication of the listeners.

Chamber Music Playing

Chamber music playing is much like solo playing in certain ways and very different in other ways. Most chamber programs that incorporate brass usually fall into two general categories. First is the program consisting entirely of brass ensemble music. Here the same considerations concerning stamina and variety that were used in formulating solo recitals should apply.

The second category is that in which brass players are performing in a mixed ensemble. Here the overriding challenge is almost always the problem of dynamic balance. In general, brass instruments played at their customary dynamic levels are somewhat too loud for other instruments. The brass player must quickly adjust to the overall dynamic context of the ensemble.

An additional challenge in any chamber performance is for the players to learn to be self-directed. The performers must be responsible for tempos, dynamics, phrasing, balance, and overall musical interpretation. This is both the great reward and the great demand of chamber ensemble performance.

Large Ensemble Playing

Finally, we will consider playing in large ensembles. Here the two principal challenges seem to be to prepare one's individual part really well and to then fit that part responsively into the larger musical milieu where one is playing. A large, conducted ensemble is really the instrument of the conductor, and the conductor's wishes guide the proceedings. Frequently the conductor's view may be different from that of the individual player. The instrumentalist's responsibility is to be stylistically and technically well prepared and responsive to the conductor's wishes.

It is absolutely essential that the individual come to the first rehearsal completely prepared. Any unprepared player wastes the rehearsal time of all the other players, and such behavior is totally unacceptable.

It is also vital that each player be willing and able to change style, tempo, dynamics, and articulation instantly at the conductor's request. Flexibility on the part of each player is crucial to the effective use of rehearsal time. This requires that every individual part be learned with the expectation of different interpretations. Rigidity has no place in good ensemble playing.

XX

Taking Auditions

Auditions are genuinely difficult experiences for most players. It should be of some comfort, however, to know that even seasoned performers usually find auditions very nerve-wracking. Young players (and older ones) should feel no shame or inadequacy simply because they find themselves very nervous. Virtually everyone goes through the same feelings to varying degrees of intensity.

It is helpful to know that many successful players have taken quite a number of auditions that they did not win. Virtually no one succeeds all the time. Auditions are highly subjective experiences, and final decisions are sometimes based on compromises. No one should deem himself a failure on the basis of an audition.

When one goes into an audition, it is important to know as much as possible about the circumstances of the position for which one is auditioning. For example, if one is auditioning in the spring (a busy auditioning time) for an orchestra, it might prove wise, in addition to any prescribed audition list, to obtain copies of the present and forthcoming years' repertory list to see what pieces of special importance to your instrument are represented. One might also be able to tell something of the conductor's predilections by the overall nature of the programming.

If specific materials are requested, those should, of course, be prepared as well as possible. Always, however, have additional appropriate material that you are prepared to play. When an auditor asks if there is anything you would like to play, be certain that you have well-chosen, well-prepared material to offer.

Although it is the music that ultimately matters most, other factors may have some influence on the final outcome of an audition. Punctuality is an absolute necessity, dress should be appropriate for the occasion, and good speaking manners and proper stage presence should be exercised.

When you are asked to play, take your time. Many nervous players rush through the designated material as if getting to the end quickly were the primary objective. Take time between selections to collect your thoughts and to focus your concentration on the music about to be played.

Most auditions provide the player the opportunity to present a solo or etude of his choosing. In auditions for teaching positions, a short recital is often requested. One of the most common errors is that people often choose music that is really at the limit of their abilities, and then in an intense situation they fall short. Remember when you have a choice to select works that show your abilities to the best advantage. A serious audition for a position you really want is not the time to try out that new, fiendishly difficult solo. Use your best, most reliable repertory. The listeners are there to judge your performance, and they are likely to be more impressed if you play very well on something less than the world's most difficult solo than if you do a poor job on a harder work. One must, of course, make selections of genuine musical worth lest both your tastes and abilities be called into question. Sound judgment includes knowing one's strengths and weaknesses.

Finally, one should not be daunted by failure or what seems to be failure. Each audition represents not only a chance to win a position but also a chance to grow, to learn more about one's craft and oneself. It is often difficult to go on after an unhappy experience, but that is precisely what needs to be done, over and over again if necessary and each time with more wisdom, experience, and confidence. The payoff will only come with proper preparation and persistence.

XXI

Playing High-Pitched Instruments

Playing high-pitched instruments such as the piccolo trumpet, the descant horn, the alto trombone, or the F tuba is a relatively recent addition to the inventory of equipment at the disposal of the modern young player. Although ownership of such equipment cannot exactly be described as commonplace, it is no longer unusual to see students, particularly at the college level, who own such instruments in addition to their regular equipment.

Modern virtuosi such as Maurice Andre, Armando Ghitalla, and Adolph Herseth have, for any who have heard them, given the piccolo trumpet credibility as a beautiful, lyrical instrument capable of producing a quality of exquisite expressiveness. Other great players have achieved comparable success on their respective instruments.

Some players, however, fail to understand the real function of such equipment, and approach it in a manner that is both musically unsatisfactory and fails to exploit the characteristics for which the instrument was created.

It is helpful, for example, if we compare the piccolo trumpet to a certain vocal quality. Similar comparisons can be made in the other members of the brass family. The piccolo is to the trumpet family as the coloratura is to the soprano genre. It is the highest, clearest (clarino) voice of the brass family, but it needs to be understood and approached as essentially vocal rather than merely as a technical apparatus to facilitate high register playing.

The physical resistance of higher pitched instruments is usually much greater than that of more commonly played equipment. Unfortunately, many players react to this resistance by using a tighter, more muscular approach to playing. The result of this increase in physical tension is a drastic reduction in airflow, and the sound produced is tight, hard, and often out of tune. Needless to say, endurance, a difficult problem in the upper registers under the best of conditions, is further reduced.

For the player who has just acquired such new equipment, I would suggest several steps for a thorough, systematic approach to learning the instrument. First, try to absorb something of the style of playing so characteristic of the best performers on the instrument. Recordings of excellent playing are numerous and readily available. Also, the player should listen to fine vocal recordings of singing in comparable registers and character that impart some of the flowing, seemingly effortless musicianship so desirable in any performing medium.

Next, allow plenty of time for playing to develop. Progress results from a combination of intelligent persistence coupled with intelligent patience. Start with a few minutes a day (and only after a thorough warm-up on your regular instrument) and slowly increase the amount of practice time. Twenty or thirty minutes a day on a small horn (assuming you use it throughout its customary playing range) is probably the equivalent in fatigue of two or three times that amount of playing on an instrument in the normal registers.

Begin by playing simple, lyrical passages. The objective is a fluid, musical line, not blazing technique. This type of playing allows the player to progress according to his or her own rate of development. Do not force the high range, and do not be anxious to develop it too rapidly. Allow time for easy natural growth to occur, both in physical strength and musical maturity. It is not enough simply to be able to play high. One also must be able to play beautifully in the most challenging of circumstances.

Next, one should work in simple étude books. At first such playing may be very tiring, but regular practice will result in increased stamina. Sizable periods of rest must be interspersed throughout the practice period.

An additional factor is that of transposition or clef reading. Players should have such experiences well in hand before beginning work on high-pitched instruments.

I would add two more specific pieces of advice for persons just beginning to play the smaller horns. First, spend a few minutes each day playing simple tunes, very easy passages, and slow, smooth scales so that you can really listen to the sounds being produced. It is easy to become so absorbed in the technical difficulties of the instrument that attention to musicality receives short shrift.

Second, pay especially close attention to intonation. Technical refinements in design and manufacturing have improved the small instruments dramatically in recent years, but the burden of good pitch still falls on the performer. Take nothing for granted. Listen constantly and critically.

Finally, perhaps the most persistent problem when playing smaller instruments is the upper register. I have only two suggestions on this matter, the first very commonplace and the second gratefully purloined from one of my teachers.

First, allow yourself time to develop. We tend to think of progress in time periods much too short. Practice regularly, skillfully, and with great concentration on fundamental musical values; that is, full, relaxed sound production, singing lines, and centered pitches. Gauge progress more in terms of weeks, months, and years than days. Most of us really do make good progress if we work at it properly, but sometimes we are too involved in our own struggles to take objective notice of our improvements. Frustration with what we take to be lack of immediate improvement often leads to the exacerbation rather than the solution of problems.

Second, learn those pieces that present truly formidable range problems on a larger instrument using the same fingerings (slide positions) and intervallic transpositions. For example, if your goal is the *Second Brandenburg Concerto* of J. S. Bach, you might wish to begin by learning it on the large B-flat trumpet using the same fingerings and transposition you would use on a B-flat piccolo. First, work out the transposition, phrasing, ornamentation, and other problems in a comfortable range (an octave lower than actually written in this case). Then move up one step by going to a C trumpet, continuing to use the same fingering patterns, then to a D trumpet and so on, until ultimately you arrive at the performance key on the proper instrument. This approach may take time, perhaps months, but it can be adjusted to individual development, and it produces more substantial progress in the end than the frustrating and sometimes damaging approach of beginning on an instrument with which one is not really familiar. Facing too many musical and technical problems at one time can be overwhelming.

The piccolo trumpet, descant horn, alto trombone, and F tuba, when approached and played properly, can be real assets. Their beautiful and distinctive qualities make these instruments virtually indispensable to modern performers.

XXII

Performance Anxiety

It is probable that every performer has experienced performance anxiety at some time during the course of a career. The question is not so much whether one experiences such sensations, but rather how and to what extent such nervousness affects playing and how one can best control and perhaps even exploit such conditions.

It should be understood at the outset that nervousness is a normal—sometimes even helpful—condition. It is the body's way of coping with situations that may be threatening. Unfortunately, physiological responses often do not discriminate between those situations that are genuinely threatening (physical danger) and those that are psychologically intimidating (public performance, job demands, etc.). Some degree of fear is a predictable, perfectly natural psychological and physical response to many unusual situations. Such situations occur regularly in nonmusical as well as musical experiences, and one can learn much about performing in public from studying those circumstances that occur in everyday living.

Moving to a new location, dealing with a serious illness or personal loss, making a public presentation, changing or losing a job, or taking a test are experiences that virtually everyone has had, and most people react with some degree of anxiousness to each of these. Each person's reaction may differ in degree and specific symptoms, but the person who has not felt some insecurity probably does not exist.

Most experiences of nervousness are linked by at least one common factor—fear of unknown circumstances. How will I do on the examination? Will the audience like my performance? Am I up to the requirements of my new job? Will the treatment for my illness be successful?

Nervousness triggers responses in all human beings, and in some fortunate people such a condition actually brings about a higher level of performance ability. Some players consistently perform better under the pressure of public scrutiny than when practicing alone. Such players seem to be the exception, however. Most people who experience stage fright find that their fear responses interfere with their ability to produce at their highest level.

What actually happens is that one's fears and insecurities, however well or ill founded, trigger certain chemical and other physiological reactions. Trembling, dry mouth, and an inability to concentrate are all common symptoms. The problem with discussing such difficulties is that each person's experiences are highly individualized, differing in degree of severity, the form of expression, and in what actual conditions stimulate such fright.

What we need to find are some common values that, if practiced and incorporated into one's work, will alleviate or at least ameliorate the fright responses.

First, it is important to understand that nervousness is normal for performers. The teacher who says to the young student, "There is nothing to be nervous about," is not only telling the student something that is not helpful; he is also telling the student something the student knows perfectly well isn't true. There *is* something to be nervous about. The student has worked hard (presumably) to prepare for a performance and is now going to display his skills for public consideration. In other words, he is risking something (his efforts, his musical reputation, etc.) that is of value to him.

What might be more appropriate would be to tell the performer that we understand the anxiety he is feeling, that it is a common one among performers, and that he should not feel as if he is somehow less capable or secure than other players just because he feels nervous. Nervousness is normal, even healthful in some circumstances, and it is common to virtually everyone.

The second step concerns how we teach ourselves and our students to deal with nervousness as a recurring condition of public performance. We should begin by emphasizing the importance of proper musical preparation. There is no substitute for the confidence that comes from knowing one can do the job. This requires long, careful, intensive and persistent work. One cannot "cram" for a performance as one might for a test in an academic subject.

Confidence in one's abilities also comes through the experience of frequent public performance. When less experienced players present a solo for the first time, they are often discouraged when the performance does not go as well as the rehearsal. In my experience I do not feel I really know a piece well until I have performed it a number of times. It is terribly important that performers play often in public. One of the great strengths of the Suzuki approach to string pedagogy is that public playing is the normal, regular, and frequent culmination of musical efforts. Players should take advantage of every opportunity for public performance, and teachers should make frequent performances a routine part of music programs. Such performances need not take the form of elaborate public concerts. Short weekly recitals at church, shopping centers, or civic clubs can be extremely valuable.

By emphasizing these three ideas—(1) that being nervous is normal, (2) that solid preparation is essential, and (3) that making frequent public appearances is important—we can go a long way toward improving the quality of performances and toward enhancing the real satisfaction that comes from making music.

XXIII

Professional Ethics

Working as a musician is a demanding occupation. Conductors, colleagues, critics, and audiences are constantly scrutinizing the performer's work. It is no small accomplishment to maintain a satisfactory balance of confidence and modesty under such scrutiny.

It is important to remember that music is what one *does*, not what one *is*. Worth as an individual is not the same as musical accomplishment. We all know scoundrels who play well and saints who do not. All players go through periods of difficulty and doubt, and it is vital for one's well being to distinguish between how well one plays and one's self worth. They are not the same.

Much of our behavior toward others is really an indication of how we feel about ourselves. The person who treats others in a respectful and pleasant manner is usually a secure individual. Genuinely confident musicians who work closely with others in very demanding situations generally exercise considerate behavior to one another.

There are four areas of professional behavior among musicians that seem to cause the most conflicts. The first is learning to communicate with one another in a nonconfrontational manner. Most people react positively when *asked* to do something in a tactful way. No one likes being *told* to do something. If we work with each other as colleagues rather than as adversaries we are all more productive. This includes conductors no less than players.

Second, players respect colleagues who are well prepared. A performer who clearly has not practiced is a detriment to the entire ensemble and has a serious effect not only on the final musical product but also on the working morale of the ensemble.

Third, personal hygiene is critical for persons who work in close physical proximity to one another. In addition to maintaining personal cleanliness, considerate persons avoid the use of strong perfumes and colognes. Some ensembles have contractual prohibitions against fragrances because of some players' allergic reactions.

Finally, be punctual! Few factors irritate others more than habitual lateness (or near lateness). Arrive at the job well prepared and in plenty of time to be ready for the service.

Most questions concerning professional behavior can be answered quite satisfactorily by simply applying the considerate, temperate behavior that every civilized person has been taught from an early age. Mutual respect and forbearance serve all our best interests.

Index